POEMS FOR PETE DAVIDSON

Ella Sadie Guthrie

ISBN: 978-1-915079-78-7

The author has asserted their right to be identified as the author of this Work in accordance with the Copyright, Designs and Patents Act 1988

Cover design by Casey Ramar - Instagram: @caseyillustration

Edited and typeset by Aaron Kent

Broken Sleep Books Ltd
Rhydwen,
Talgarreg,
SA44 4HB
Wales

Contents

Poems for Pete Davidson

Ella Sadie Guthrie

pete davidson (ariana grande could never)

recently i've been daydreaming of pete davidson

this is not unordinary   they come to me like woodlouse

crawling out of piles of damp leaves onto the knees of late school children

my daydreams are not jabberwockys caning cans of red bull, much simpler, instead

on one hour walks i look at wooden tables leaning against closed pubs think *hmmm*

if i happened to run into pete davidson on this street corner would we

fall in love with a badly delivered joke over a glass of soda and lime?

would we sit outside, oblivious to onlookers scouring my hands for seven rings?

how long would it take for opportunists with cameras to get lucky?   i can see it

my head turned in slight shock, he, a library statue, all knowledge

in my newest fantasy i am wearing sunglasses that don't hide my face

and he is pale, so pale the sun decides to shine on him directly like a detective's desk lamp

　　　'what do you do in the shadows?' it asks

i tell the sun to soften on his features and offer him factor 50

he is grateful i am the good cop

later, i walk along brighton beach, lick my lips between waves retching on the shoreline

and play this image in my head over and over again

my feet the mechanism transforming my eyelids into a private cinema

audio playing 'this is okay' with too much fervour to be wholesome

when i go home i hesitate to write this down

what if one day he sees this poem?

my woodlouse fantasies, childish and toxic like a chalkboard

his ex wrote the song 'pete davidson' in the whirlpool of their relationship

now she is married to someone else i can't help but hope he is not clinging to the side of his life
        wishing for armbands

pete, i whisper to the other side of the dark   *don't drown*

i will be your lifeguard

and halfway across the world on the light side of the moon

he drifts off and i sing

pete davidson is getting his tattoos removed

and i worry i will no longer find him sexy

until i laugh myself into next week and remember

the obsession has less to do with his sex appeal and more

with my longing for soft pretzels and posh raspberry berets at press parties

yes, i hate myself for this need to feel validated

but it doesn't make me need it less

i would sell my body to the harpies in the seventh circle of hell

if it meant i could sit opposite patti on a poetry panel

this self flagellation is more embarrassing

than professing my love for a non-tattooed pete davidson because

yes, he is attractive in a strange way and yes, he probably triggers my

child-of-alcoholic response to smother him with a stable relationship

and yes, his lack of tattoos will make it easier to introduce him to my family

digest roast chicken with cold judgement at the dinner table

but it's also to do with the fact that i am clinging to the fantasy of

reading my book aloud on the strand, making him laugh with my words

pete davidson has a new girlfriend

and i am cutting my teeth on new poetry collections to make me seem sharper

i am happy for him don't get me wrong

but i am also banging my head on the chopping board
        telling my mother it's the onions

it's not that i am heartbroken

on the contrary, i regularly pray for his heart to find a regular pattern

and not flatline into coping mechanisms

but now i will have to parallel park the highly developed sensory landscapes
        confined to the corner of my mind unused unless in emergencies like

rearranging the furniture i saved for our first brooklyn apartment and

at this moment
        butterflies start to make short-lived homes among the fuchsias in the front garden

dolphins breach fresh mackerel onto worn pebbles and i am in love

with the way nature carves its name into each day

oh suck me through a puddle and turn my fingertips into fresh dates!

i don't have enough space in my brain
        to learn someone new's favourite colour or particular parental dynamics

save me the internet searches
        don't remind me there's a world out there

i cannot feign interest in another episode of the joe rogan podcast

and now my fantasy world is turning itself to dust with the realisation that my crush has a real love

so i close the door to my head for a bit, try to remember every woman's face on the train platform

sometimes i worry
        everyone else's hopes and dreams are so much lighter than mine

pete davidson and i share coffee in a new york diner

closer to good morning than good night

        those small numbers that feel both alive and dying
we sit with black coffee, stale toast and forgo small talk

i tell him
        ask me big questions, ones that keep you awake at night

have you ever asked the ceiling if it's met the sky?

in this daydream, delicate and liquid in its immaculate conception

i am in new york shooting a movie from a script i haven't yet adapted

too busy bending myself into fixtures of london furniture and judging a scene i helped create but
in my daydream i am

        playing patti smith in just kids, wrapping my teeth around the word yellow
        like a greek prayer

cheers to the life we live pete,

we crash cheap china together, careless in our rush of adrenaline

we are here by chance
        everyone famous in new york knows everyone

pete and i meet at a party neither of us wanted to be invited to, irish exit to an all night eatery, an
old jukebox bacon and eggs at any time of day

i am skinny, hollywood skinny, this is a significant part of the daydream

i am playing patti penniless and passionate
        funny, only loving men has ever made me this thin

he is cascading down the side of the walls with jokes
                that scrape the sides of societies melting pot

i am laughing, cold coffee breath, already in love

the jukebox plays harvest moon by neil young
                    i have imagined dancing to this at my wedding
he takes my hand

for once no one cares who we are, invisible
a metal detector casing sand and coming up dry

nighthawks inventing new stories to play in

pete davidson is single again

and i am obsessed with not checking the internet so that his image can live pristine

in my head we have found each other and it is beautiful like that fred again track i wish i could have made

the one with the poet at the bus station who found the girl
        that fred discovered pierced his heart just enough to echo the voice in the music

in my head we meet and we kiss in an improvised jazz soundscape made of yelling and jackhammers and all the words one human could ever say to another one

this is new york, of course
        and this is the most unrealistic part of the daydream

because i cannot find myself in an america restricted by covid and capitol storming and environmental crises

today, a south londoner won her first-ever us open at 18 and when she smiles all i can see in her face is my sister, carefree and happy and imagine being that good at anything

dedicating life to anything but maladaptive daydreaming that is contagious to my concentration

i write down through smokey chaos
        and listen to more successful artists talk about music taste on radio 6

today is 9/11 or as we say in the uk 9/11 and whilst i am mourning the loss of millions of people and explaining to my mother that buildings don't fall like that i am thinking of pete davidson

hoping he is coping with the realisation that the last twenty years of his life he has been fatherless

and i want to reach through the thousands of miles distance between us and all the degrees of separation and tell him i'm sorry for his loss

hold my arms like a ballerina mimicking al dente spaghetti around his pale body
and let him create a sea of starch water around us

this is his spinning moment, circus sick and shaky

yet still my fantasy

pete davidson is the king of staten island

and whilst watching this debut
          i become increasingly more uncontrollable in my jealousy that i was born on the wrong
side of the world

he's a scorpio too, i tell my mother weeping with the lateness of the evening

i do the maths i am twenty two days older than him, but we know he loves a cougar so my muscles
soften into the sofa

i imagine how he'd post about me on my thirtieth birthday if he had instagram

i would hide my face as he danced to 'older lady' by masego, but i'm loving it, you can tell

i google the actors in the film and one of them is british

my belly falls over itself tripping on a loose wire imagining all the figs i could have eaten

will poetry ever pay? will it ever really matter?

the moment my head hits the pillow tonight i will think about how each fig has only been allowed
to blossom because a wasp has sacrificed itself
          dying in the closing petals of a flower

only to be repurposed into soft pastry and plastic wrapping

what kind of sick world is it where i can eat a whole packet of fig rolls and conjure up images of us together

asleep, i am a magician and pete davidson is a white, white rabbit
                              freshly caught and too domesticated to run away

i watch the film again, memorising the madness behind his eyes, damp in an oversized paddling pool
                    and i laugh

because it's written to be funny

i am laughing as singing your lover's favourite advert jingle

to take a breathe after resurfacing from the deepest part of a natural rock pool

as in you cannot fail to do so
          when someone has worked this hard at creating joy out of grief

16

pete davidson and i meet in a crowded bar

we are in manchester because i know he has been here before

and my daydreams are nothing if not attentive to the details of realism

i am working on a poem, which is for once
                                    not about him

and he asks me about it

so i describe to him how the universe can be kaleidoscopic and monochrome all at once and he laughs

in a subtle way to let me know he understands

a hand reaching for your finger in a room where the lights go out suddenly and you need to know at least one person won't murder you

my hair is in a ponytail and we make small talk on the type of high stools no one really wants to sit at

our backs curving to gravity and the weight of my expectation

i drink whiskey and he doesn't, because in my daydreams i believe him

and we leave the bar together

deciding where and how far to go

pete davidson and i meet at a new york comedy show

i am in new york for the fun of it

and he is incognito at a new material night

i stand up on stage and tell everyone i am not a comic

this is supposed to be funny

remember, this is a fantasy, so in this scenario i read monica by hera lindsay bird

except i am hera lindsay bird, and everyone laughs, because this poem is hilarious

and at the end pete comes up to me
        to tell me how funny i am and i hide the deception with a wry smile

i forget i did not really write this poem   all the songs i play again and again and again
frying each individual wire in my brain *i did not write them*

and there it is again, that funny feeling
        that takes me away from the daydream and into the downward spiral of dissociation and
all this time i spend inhaling the smoke and drinking my own kool aid

pete is standing there   still as the first dandelion of spring holding a joint the way a dove
holds an olive branch in the bible

and i accept though i don't smoke weed

this makes him laugh and i blush with the pride of simping

for the only man left i would giggle for

come back to my apartment
                                    he says

there's a fire escape begging for you to dream on it

pete davidson and i meet in a hip new art gallery near brooklyn

i've never actually been to brooklyn so i can't describe the surroundings, or the street or tell you which letter train i look to get there but i can tell you it is raining outside and i am big black boots and dungarees

and everyone in the art gallery is careful to hold each other's expectations in the centre of the room desperate don't accidentally alter priceless pieces

in this scenario my hair is long, dark and dripping wet

i never remember my umbrellas and i left my hat holding onto a rope
the kind that could break at any moment when i look into the mirror and see my real reflection

i am wearing a long grey coat by ralph lauren i got for free from a girl who left her flat in camberwell for singapore at late notice
        (in real life i lost the coat a couple of years ago)

but here i am - an island in its waters
        reminding myself the good things always come back

pete davidson stands alone, for once

he is admiring a piece of art projected onto the wall
the piece builds the longer you stare at it
at first, you don't notice the small alterations
        the offering of each layer   a mother in law slowly adding more sugar to your tea

a whole conversation passes before we look at the art again and see a totally different escape

wet wood, an hourglass, a dog waiting for its owner to come home

i see none of these things and yet i feel them in the absence of what came before

i say nothing

it reminds me of the joan miro museum at the top of monjuric, barcelona
        where i spent the whole day contorting myself into thinly veiled paintings of dicks

i tell him this, he laughs

pete davidson is playing johnny ramone

and it reminds me that i wanted to get singing lessons to fulfil my other fantasy

patti smith and phoebe bridgers and the chelsea hotel

poetry and practice and spirits banishing stage fright

there are only so many times you can pretend to have written hayley williams' entire discography

and imagine singing happier than ever in the face of your ex lover until you throw up all the lyrics

ever written into the bowl of a cheap ukulele

as a child i would shut out the world by running the length of my corridor

i need the movement of my feet for my eyes to think

i haven't grown out of this except now i use the south coast to break down

and listen to the sound of a woman's voice telling a story so similar to how i feel

it's all i can do

without sinking into the void

pete davidson and i get married

cue the church bells and the white dress

cue the tabloids printing every headline

cue the bets on how long it will last

i couldn't care less, i am wearing silk in spain

and my husband kisses me like i am oxygen as we cut a cake

made out of glitter and carnations because fuck it why not

sugar is a plastic fish nailed to the wall

only love could touch every part of the tongue on this day

delicate and dackering in the neo liberalism of our union

yellow dressed dappled light, sparkling water fountain suits

sit on tongues like bees resting on a flower

phoebe bridgers and tom misch play the first song

and they cover harvest moon so beautifully

silk chiffon teeth, eyes like forest fires

there is not a dry eye in the house

i wake with a wet face

pete davidson returns to snl

this time the rumour mill ran out of flour and started breaking bread with the sandstone of the hillside

everyone cut their teeth on their sandwiches, filled with the tongues of anyone who has ever read perez hilton

how wrong we can be about each other
gossip rots like the carcass of a fox on a train track

i've never belly laughed at saturday night live but it fills my sunday evenings as i peel potatoes

pete davidson has been on this program since his 21st year
        i am two weeks older than him and the only time i've entered the studio is in daydreams

amber and soft in their edges

my hair longer, my smile whiter, my body smaller, more compact

my voice not held down by stage fright

in the disney version of the little mermaid ariel wins and ursula becomes food for the bottom feeders

disney has always wrapped the danger in diabetes
        a spoonful of medicine to wash the racism down

in the real story ariel dies voiceless and alone

ursula gets the man, gets to whisper melodically into his ear for all eternity

no consequences, just a beautiful voice and a happy ending

watching the sun rise from the small window in my bedroom again and again
        maybe i'd trade my soul for the bliss of a happy ending

with no repercussions

pete davidson is pictured holding hands with kim k

i am getting serious about poetry and cursing the flesh around my abdomen in the hope it may
one day stretch to protect a child

my womb a cluster of spiders spinning silk swaddles for a baby that may never come

my mother says 'when' and i correct her to 'if'   i don't drool over a family life

      there is no way i can tell what this saliva drenched future will hold

      it will probably involve a water shortage

i study the picture silently, my head a dark cave, a drip soaking one small piece of my throat as a
source describes them as friends

is that what my friendships look like? captured and crystallised in fear and fun
a satsuma preserving each kiss on the cheek in one drop of juice
the way i only feel validated when i am held

on mushrooms i look for orange light to bathe in
      wonder if each individual wrong turn will eventually lead to my undoing

rock me to sleep on a canopy of poisonous oak
      is this a bassinet or a ship plunging to the bottom of the seabed?

my life, another wreck examined by a team of scientists
      white gloves and relationship dramas cutting open the rotting bough of my stomach
pull me apart and the fish who have made homes in my bones run to find a new place to nest

      i can bet one will wrap around my intestines turned return to earth green
and the scientists will laugh, not careful with the scalpel

sometimes i wake up in the middle of the night scared i am plunging too deep into debt
      i distract myself with the names of future children i may never have

whenever i imagine my children i conveniently leave out chicken pox and tantrums in supermarkets
instead i think about the way their first breath would feel against the peach of my skin, how it could
be possible to love someone that much, a heart on fire and hopelessly ignorant of it

      imagining these things is to pour salt water on a wound that needs iodine

once again i put my hand on my stomach and imagine the possibility of a sapling
pink and bloody in its immaculacy the impossibility and yet mundaneness of it

i fall further out of love with the idea there could ever be a god
what is a womb if not a cardboard box full of longing and hope and fear

if i think hard enough i can imagine his hand
not pixelated on news sites, but on on the slight curve of my flesh

warm and heavy
         his pulse radiating through his thumb, pressed into the side of my ribs

pete davidson and i have a son

and i can't print what we name him in case we ever do have a son and it's tarnished by these twisted khaki thoughts

run through tough mud and churned up on winter mornings

this is how deeply deluded i am

this hope circulates my head when i cannot move it from the pillow

my friend asks where i get the energy to dream all these things

i fire depression at him with finger guns

we laugh

pete davidson mourns my death

i have always dreamed of dying
                not the dying itself, but the afterbirth, the wetness wallow of it

how broken and sad everyone would be once i'm gone

how they would season the earth with their sorrow,
                              write opinion pieces, share my poems on social media
plant sunflowers on windowsill allotments

gone too soon, hashtag rip

how many offerings would be brought to my funeral, how devastated my husband would be,
clinging to our young son like an armband in the ocean
                                  allergic to the way history repeats itself

i would haunt him forever, watch our son write me into his own fantasies

touch his shoulder in pure energy

i am not trying to manifest this, rather there is a type of pleasure in knowing for certain that
someone cares enough to live for you long after the body is returned to organic matter

and i've always felt i would die young

die beautiful, die a hero for the arts, my picture painted as a mural and washed away by the sea

but i am already 27 and if i were to not wake up tomorrow my words would be nothing but daisies

dead before the summer is even over
                          club membership denied, you have to have achieved something
                                              anything
to join amy and jimmy and all their friends

i often ask myself if the offer were etched into an oak table in the early hours of the morning
carved with the butt of a cigarette i vowed never to smoke again

if i would give up my life in ten years time
                                      go willingly to hell

leave pete davidson and our little boy wiping away tears from raw skin
                        alone in the wake of the cold and empty days in exchange

for a memorial live streamed to the living rooms of grieving fans

                                        i would tell you i could never be that cruel

but if the chance came

i make pete davidson on sims 4

i play it for four days straight

until the original sims are dead and all that's left is a legacy of pixelated people with names that sound sophisticated

i have already used up all the names i think would suit an amalgamation of us so i google all names that begin with s, soft and stuck and simple in its sophistication

santiago, the boy who could harness the wind
        sacrum, the bone that holds history
                sadist, the dark label to dip into when the night finds its way to earth

this fake town is getting too small for all the fake people i am making but i can't stop making them fuck each other until they collapse from exhaustion

pete davidson is now a ghost and occasionally comes back to haunt his grandchildren who he's never met

i have a ghost in my head that penetrates underneath my eyebrows
        when i finally go to sleep i dream we are sims living in sim city

and all my daydreams come true in the night until the city collapses into thousands of breezeblocks

we turn into aliens and the hell is real billboards pollute the sky in pastels and screaming

it falls on me as i clutch pete davidson, but he evaporates just as i wake up

birdsong falling into a crescendo from my phone at the foot of the bed

pete davidson dies and i mourn his death

o, the revelry of it
        the parade and the pagentery

tell me why i am desperate to know this kind of finality
and wake up suffocating my imagination, dripping with salt, sweat and thick guilt

how has this always been the straw that sent the old lady crying into the ocean
craving grief like a kiss on the forehead to cure a migraine

the image distorts, as if wrapped in sellotape and shame
i write music for the love i lost, four chords and a folk melody
a love song / a murder ballad

this is no nightmare
i am the architect of this, hand shaking holding the pen
how easily the ink falls out of it, a peacock sacrificing itself for the slaughter

i have gone too far this time
        each morning that turns into an afternoon with my mind cocooned in fat fantasy is another
nail in my coffin

take a deep breath and walk away from the dirges

the music i didn't write gets quieter, replaced with familiar rhythm

i can, i can, i can

wake up
start living.

Notes

P.9 - pete davidson (ariana grande could never) first published in Lucent Dreaming magazine, issue 9.

P.15 - The song referenced is by Fred Again and is called Kyle (I Found You).

P.16 - 'pete davidson is the king of staten island' is in reference to 'The King Of Staten Island' (2020). Dir. Judd Appatow, Writ. Pete Davidson, Judd Appatow, Dave Sirus.

P. 18 - 'pete davidson and i meet at a new york comedy show' references the poem Monica by Hera Lindsay Bird, which can be found in her collection 'Hera Lindsay Bird'.

P. 20 - 'happier than ever' is a reference to the song by Billie Eilish.

P. 26 - 'to join amy and jimmy and all their friends' is in reference to Amy Winehouse, James Morrisson and the 27 Club.

Acknowledgements

When I told people I was going to write this book, many of them asked if I was ok. But the truth is this has been one of the most cathartic writing experiences of my life. Ever since I was a child I have lived in my head, daydreaming scenarios and experiences alongside my favourite book and film characters that I would forget to live in the real world. I would beat myself up for these long periods of time I 'wasted', wondering how 'successful' I would be if I weren't plagued by the never ending cinema reel in my mind. So, I decided to write about it. My reasoning was that if I could make art out of the daydreams, maybe it wouldn't be such a waste. What emerged was an exploration of my own psyche, ADHD, celebrity culture and why oh why I love Pete Davidson so much. Turns out it's more what he represents; New York, Writing, Comedy, Poetry, Love, Fame and that dreaded noun, Success. Through this pamphlet I've worked hard to dispel a lot of the ideas I've had on these subjects, coming to terms and putting to rest Pete as a concept in the process. If you bought this book, if you read it, thank you. I hope you enjoyed going down the rabbit hole with me.

There are many people I have to thank. Firstly, Aaron Kent and Broken Sleep, for taking a chance on a very weird collection of poems. I feel so priveleged to have my first proper book out with you. Thank you Fern Beattie for being the one to suggest it, you believed before even I did. Thank you to Jannat Ahmed for giving the first Pete Davidson poem a home in Lucent Dreaming, that acceptance email turned one poem into twenty.

Thank you to the wonderful Casey Ramar for the beautiful illustration on the front cover, for somehow being able to read my mind and turning it into the coolest book I've ever seen.

Thank you to Ollie O'Neill, my poetry wife, my words by the water collaborator and dear cherished friend, I would not be the poet I am today without your wisdom.

Thank you to Ruth Boon, my other poetry wife, my co-starter of wriots and one of my favourite and the most hilarious poets to ever live. I am a better person for your friendship.

To the rest of my WRIOT crew, Charlotte Shevchenko Knight, Scarlett Ward-Bennett, Romy Foster, Maheni Arthur, Daphne Smith, Rachel Lewis, Rachel Cleverly, Constance Richardson, Rosie Burke, Olivia Atkins. Thank you for your continued support.

To PJ, AKA The Repeat Beat Poet, thank you for dragging me on stage for the first time and telling me I could do it if I wanted. To Jeremiah Brown, AKA Sugar J for telling me writing poems would only make me a better writer overall, thank you Cecilia Knapp for writing the kinds of poems that inspired me to write my own. Thank you to Hera Lindsay Bird for writing 'Monica' which made me realise I could write surreal bizzare poems about celebrity culture and maybe be taken seriously in literature.

Thank you to anyone who has ever graced the stage of Words By The Water and the lovely team at Selina for allowing us to hold it there.

Thank you to Dakota Blue Richards, for reading all my poems whether they were good or not, for listening to all my weird fantasies and for allowing me to have my weird celebrity crush even though you never understood the hype. You'll never be dead to me.

Thank you Eleni Mettyear for being my personal photographer, for feeding me and for giving me advice I'm not always ready to take. Thank you to Ellie Alford for understanding my crush, Tori Rodway and Maddy Brooks for being amazing women that inspire me so much. Meli for all your voicenotes about why loving Pete is okay. Dannie for being the people's princess of my poetry.

It seems silly that a little book like this would have so many people to thank, but I'd also like to say a big appreciate you to Lauryn Foord, Lebby Leeding, Bec and Matt Andrews, Lucy Guthrie, Lars Thornhill, Kit Nicholas, Ali Woods, Alice Tingey, Lucy Skoulding, Kirsty Hobson, Sabrina Miller, Nash, Natz and Jak Hutchcraft, Phil Wilcox, Marged Sion, Melissa Morrison, Lonan Jenkins, Sol and Alex Bowra, Imogen Tindale, Nabeela Singh, Jay McDougal, Ben Duke, Harry Jay Robinson, Mel and Annie Stevens, Laurie Mayhew, Lisa Smith, Ed Riman, Emily Brown, Bryony White, Jessie Brooks, Lewis Kay Thatcher, Pandora Hall, Mario Lottari, Tommy Burley, Romana Imi, and all the beautiful friends in my life I may have forgotten to list. You've all inspired me at some point along the way and for that I'm eternally grateful.

To my family, my mum, Kerrie Guthrie for always believing in me even in the worst of times, my dad Micky. My grandad Raymond Smith for passing on your love of jazz and my little sister Meg Guthrie for bringing out the best and worst in me.

Lastly, thank you to Pete Davidson, especially the fake version of you I created in my mind, without whom none of this would be possible. If you happen to be reading this, call me.

LAY OUT YOUR UNREST

www.ingramcontent.com/pod-product-compliance
Lightning Source LLC
Chambersburg PA
CBHW081553040426
42448CB00016B/3310

* 9 7 8 1 9 1 5 0 7 9 7 8 7 *